Teach Your Dog 9 Commands in 9 Days:

A Simple Obedience Starter Guide

by Shel Gatto

ISBN: 978-1478222293

A big thank you to my wonderful husband Allan who helped capture many of the images used in this guide.

Table of Contents

Bonding through Obedience Training

Guiding your dog through obedience training can be a very rewarding experience. Whether you just adopted a puppy or have had your beloved pet for 10 years, it is always a good time to work on basic training. The process takes patience and effort, so be prepared to invest energy into multiple short sessions each day.

There are many commands that you can teach your pet depending on your primary focus and purpose. This guide will not get into advanced specialized skills. It will show you how to lay a solid foundation with basic commands that are necessary to move on to complex tricks and abilities. You will find simple commands that keep your pet safe and under control as well as a couple that make great conversation starters.

Not all canines learn at the same pace. It is possible to teach your dog one of the nine commands included in this guide per day. Keep each training session shorter rather than longer, with reduced sessions if your dog is still a young puppy.

Staying under the 15 minute mark will help make each session more fruitful for you and your pet. Try to fit in three to five training sessions per day and adjust based on your dog's response and attention span.

Do not become frustrated if your pet has difficulty grasping one or two of the concepts explained here. He or she will get it in time, so be patient and remember that successful dog training relies on the human also being well-trained. Often times a dog's inability to learn lies with the way he or she is being taught. Pay close attention and adjust to your pet's learning abilities so you can glide through these nine commands and move on advanced training sessions. Good luck!

Mixed breed Thibor waits patiently during training

Chapter 1
Before You Begin Obedience Training

Before you begin your first training session, make sure you have a few items available. The following list will help you prepare for all nine commands. You may not need all items for each command, but it is best to have them on hand so you are ready to go each day!

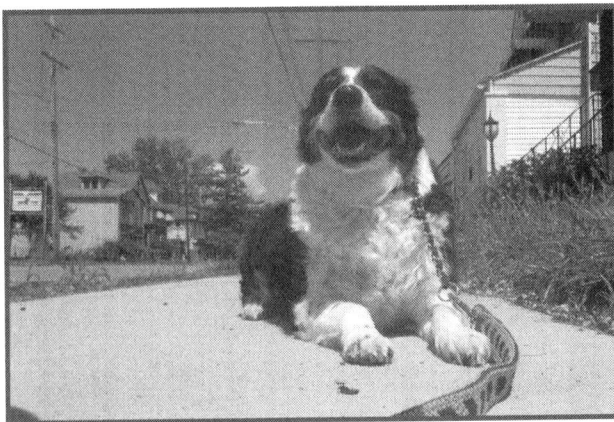

English shepherd Nathan rests after a walk

The Short Lead

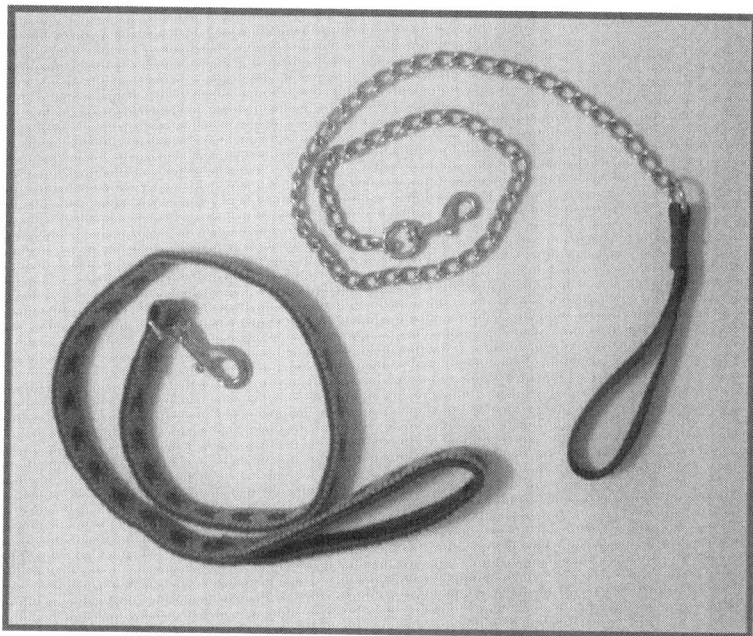

Examples of nylon (left) and chain (right) short leads

A short lead will be necessary when teaching the heel command. Think of the type of leash you would normally walk your dog with. It should be no more than five or six feet in length. You can use a longer lead in place of a short lead, but be prepared to hold on to the excess slack when working on commands that require a short lead.

I do not recommend using a retractable leash for training. The retractable design makes it difficult to react quickly and keep your hands in the proper position during training. While it is possible to use one, it may get in the way.

When choosing a short lead, make sure it is one that you are comfortable holding. You will need to hold it in two spots for some training sessions. A nylon lead may be easier to grip than a chain lead.

Your pet's size and energy level will also come into play here. This is vital when teaching the "heel" command because some dogs pull at first and you may find yourself gripping the middle of the lead firmly to stay in control and correct the behavior.

A chain can be painful to grip if your pet is very strong and pulls frequently. Try a strong nylon leash or wear work gloves to protect your hands until your pet learns proper leash etiquette. This will not likely be an issue with a smaller dog or one that doesn't pull hard to begin with.

Nathan practices stay while on a walk

The Long Lead

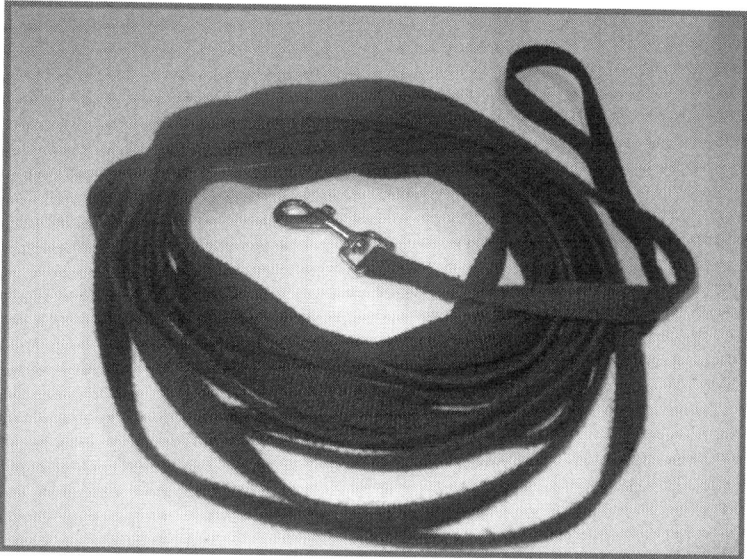

Example of an inexpensive nylon long lead

A long lead should be at least 15 feet, however over 20 to 30 feet is even better. This gives you the chance to safely reinforce commands at a distance. A long lead is vital when working on the "stay" command in an outdoor setting.

If you plan to handle training in your home, then the long lead may not be necessary because your dog will not be able to get away and get into trouble. It is highly recommended that you take your pet to an outdoor setting to reinforce obedience in all situations once he or she has mastered commands indoors. This practice will require the use of a long lead.

Your Voice

Your voice is a free training tool that you will use in every single session. You may not realize it, but the volume and tone of your voice influences the effectiveness of training. Dogs read body language and process the way you say things along with what you are saying.

Do not scream or yell at your dog when training. Instead, use a calm tone and keep volume at a normal speaking level. When praising, you can use higher pitched tones but maintain the same volume. Remember to emphasize your praise with happy words and sounds. Praise is not effective if you give it in an unenthusiastic or monotone voice.

If you frequently shout at your dog, then he or she will come to expect this. Your pet will essentially get used to it and may not respond to what you are saying. It can be easy to get frustrated and raise your voice, but keep your sounds in check. Your dog doesn't speak English and wants to please you, but you have to make communication as clear as possible.

Also remember that you must use the same command phrase or word each time. If you switch words or phrases for a command, your pet may become confused. Most dogs can learn basic variations of a command, but this is not recommended when teaching the command for the first time. You do not have to use the exact phrases noted in this guide for each command, however keep it as simple as possible.

Optional Tool: Hand Gestures

Dogs can learn to respond to hand gestures just as effectively as they respond to voice commands. This is an optional step, but if you plan to utilize gestures then make sure you accompany them with your spoken commands.

For example, it is easy to teach your pet to "sit" when you point your index finger to the ground in front of you. Make the gesture as you teach your pet the spoken "sit" command. As your dog associates the spoken command with the proper response, he or she will also associate the gesture.

Make sure you have decided on the hand gesture before using it to avoid confusing your pet. Just like voice commands, if you switch gestures midway through training, he or she may not understand what you are trying to say.

It is possible to teach hand gestures later, after your pet knows the spoken version of a command. You do not have to add this step yet. If you are just starting out with canine obedience training, then it may be easier to work with voice commands only then add gestures later.

To show your pet the hand gesture version of a command he or she already knows, simply make the gesture and speak the command. Reward your pet for the proper response and repeat a number of times. Then begin performing the gesture only, without the command.

If your pet doesn't understand, return to the voice and gesture combination until you get your pet to complete the action with just the gesture. Make sure you praise and reward vigorously when your pet finally makes the connection as soon as the proper response is achieved.

Optional Tool: The Clicker

The clicker is a popular training tool that comes highly recommended. It utilizes positive reinforcement to communicate with your pet. The clicker is extremely simple to use and easy to condition your dog to. It is not necessarily a requirement when training, but it can help streamline the process and give you a quick way to let your pet know when he or she is on the right path.

Most pet supply stores sell clickers for a dollar or two, so it is well worth the investment. You don't need anything fancy, a simple clicker with one or two click settings will suffice for basic obedience training.

How to Use the Clicker

Using a clicker is extremely easy, even for a beginner. The concept of the clicker revolves around getting your pet to associate the subtle *click* the device makes with positive reinforcement. Once your pet has learned what the sound means it will be much easier to guide him or her through basic obedience training.

To use most clickers, simply push down on the exposed metal plate with your thumb. Some newer clickers have a button to press instead. The end result is essentially the same: a single click is heard.

Many clickers have a small slider that lets the owner choose a different tone for the click. This can be helpful in advanced obedience training or when working with multiple dogs in a shared classroom. For the basic commands in this guide, you will only need to utilize one setting.

Timing the click is going to be the biggest challenge for a new dog trainer. A series of clicks can confuse the dog so make sure you get into the habit of pressing just once. Only click when your dog is taking the proper action. If you click too soon, the dog will learn that whatever action is being taken at that moment is the correct response. If you click too late, the same will result.

After buying a new clicker, give it a try prior to training. This will allow you to feel how much pressure must be applied to make it click before you attempt to use it to communicate with your dog.

Always reward as soon as you click. If you wait several seconds, even to fish a treat out of your pocket, the moment may be lost on your dog. He or she may think it is just a treat rather than a reward for a correct response. It can help to have a treat or two in your hand or in an open pouch on your belt so you can quickly grab the treat and give it to the dog as soon as the click is issued. The quicker you are to click and reward, the faster your pet will learn. The same goes for praise rewards.

Optional Tool: The Choke Chain

Example of a choke chain with a nylon weave

The choke chain is a touchy subject with some pet owners, and it is understandable why many would be reluctant to use them. The choke chain provides a way to correct your pet when he or she is not obeying commands. The problem with choke chains is that when not used properly, they can be harmful to your pet physically and behaviorally.

I recommend the choke chain for pet owners with strong and/or high energy level dogs who are unruly or difficult to handle, especially when on a lead. This tool *can* be used safely and effectively. The goal should be to use the choke chain minimally and improve your pet's behavior so you rarely have to correct with the choke chain after basic obedience training.

Some dogs will eventually get to the point where it is not needed while others may take longer. The situation will vary from one dog to the next. The following section will discuss the proper way to use the choke chain so you and your pet can keep each training session as positive and effective as possible.

There are multiple choke chain varieties available. The basic type consists of a single length of chain with two large metal loops at each end. Some include a weave of nylon or fabric that helps prevent tangles and pulling when used on long haired canines. The type pictured in this guide is a basic choke chain with the protective nylon weave.

Large, powerful canines may require a choke chain with thicker links or one with teeth. Follow the weight and breed recommendations listed by the manufacturer when choosing a choke chain for your pet.

Proper Choke Chain Use

Using a choke chain properly isn't as easy as slipping it on your dog's neck and pulling. In fact this can have the opposite effect on your pet's ability to learn. The choke chain can be a valuable tool, especially if your dog pulls frequently on the leash. Always utilize the choke chain in the correct way to avoid hurting your pet.

A choke chain ready for training

To prepare the choke chain, feed slack through one of the metal rings so that it rests around the chain itself as seen in the image above. The free end can be secured to a lead. This will form a complete loop that will automatically shrink or expand each time you tug or allow slack. A choke chain should never be used to tie a dog outside or anywhere that doesn't include you holding the lead because it allows for this type of adjustment.

The chain should be slipped over your dog's head and placed high up on the neck. The higher up it is the more control you will have. An elevated position also reduces the amount of force needed when applying a correction. Some dogs can actually get used to pulling when the chain sits too low on the neck. If you feel as though you are pulling very hard to keep your dog under control, then the choke chain may be sitting too low.

Left: A properly positioned choke chain
Right: A choke chain that hangs too low

Make sure the choke chain does not become wrapped around your dog's collar. Some wide collars can prevent the chain from working because they stop the pulling motion. The dog should feel pressure when he or she attempts to yank, which discourages the movement. If the dog's regular collar interferes, then he or she will continue to pull.

Nathan practices heel while on a walk

Do not remove your dog's collar when training outdoors. This most likely has his or her tags attached to it which will be necessary if your pet should accidentally escape. Instead, make sure the choke chain and collar do not overlap. It is best to keep the collar lower on the neck so the choke chain can sit comfortably right where it needs to.

When you need to give a correction with the choke chain, one quick tug upwards or to the side should do the trick. This should not be viewed as a painful punishment. Instead it is intended to snap your dog's attention back to you. Start with light tugs and only increase force if your pet does not respond. View this type of correction as a way to say "Hey, look at me!" rather than a way to hurt your pet.

Never walk your dog on a lead with significant tension. The choke chain should be pulled snugly around the dog's neck, but not tight. Your pet should barely feel it when you are not applying a correction. Avoid allowing the chain to hang too loose as well. Too much slack can let your dog to slip his or her head out of the choke chain. This can also unintentionally reposition the choke chain and delay your response time when applying a correction.

Just like you must be quick with the clicker, you must also be quick with the choke chain. Only give a swift tug when your dog is in the process of doing something wrong. Correcting after the fact will confuse your pet.

Optional Tool: Dog Treats and Food Rewards

Dog treats are a great way to reward your canine, as long as they are used sparingly. Too many treats can lead to two main problems: the expectation of food when responding to a command and obesity. Believe it or not your dog can get fat on too many treats, especially if you award them frequently.

You can get away with using positive praise and petting as a reward for your pet. Some dogs are much more responsive to a food reward. Try mixing the two by giving praise for smaller achievements and rewarding your pet for each bigger step forward with a treat.

For example, if your pet is moving in the right direction you can keep him or her going with lots of upbeat praise. When he or she finally executes the command successfully, give a treat as a reward along with more petting and praise.

Avoid predictable treat and reward patterns. Make sure you are giving treat rewards randomly so your dog stays interested throughout each training session. You can sneak one or two in between praise if necessary to boost canine motivation.

Also remember that a treat doesn't have to be a whole dog biscuit. Consider cutting treats up into small pieces. This will cost far less because a whole box or bag of treats will go much further and it will keep your pet's food intake at healthy levels.

Some dog owners chop up cheese, apples or bits of meat in place of biscuits. If you plan to give a food reward, choose something that is healthy for your dog. Make sure you reduce the size of each treat as necessary so your pet isn't receiving more servings than he or she should each day.

The Classroom

Dogs are generally adaptable animals. They don't really mind where you train them, as long as the right conditions exist. You can take your pet into a large closet, the bathroom, your bedroom, the garage, anywhere as long as the space and conditions exist to nurture his or her obedience education. If you live in a small house, apartment or a household with many others, then you may need to find an out of the way place to begin training.

An ideal dog classroom will include an area that is quiet and distraction-free. Eventually you can take your pet somewhere with distractions to reinforce what he or she has learned, but when you start out you must keep your pet's focus on you. Loud noise, activity, voices and toys in the area will make it that much harder to get your dog to listen and pay attention.

Whether your classroom is indoors or outdoors doesn't really matter. When utilizing an outdoor space, make sure you have control over the nearby area. Ideally this might be a fenced in yard or secluded area that others don't visit often. Also remember that other animals, such as neighborhood cats or birds, could wander into the area and cause a distraction.

Choose a space that is quiet and safe for your dog. With that in mind, you can also plan for additional training locations that include more noise and activity when you take your pet to the next level of obedience training.

Chapter 2
Teaching the Touch Command

Touch is extremely valuable when moving your pet into advanced commands. It is also relatively easy to teach. This command tells your pet to "touch" your palm with his or her nose. The action sounds basic, but it allows you to easily position your dog.

Australian Shepherd Caladesi waits for the touch command

Step 1

Give the touch command with your palm or hand held out towards your dog. Do not place your palm up against his or her nose. Make sure your pet has to actually move at least a few inches to touch your hand.

Caladesi performs touch from a distance

Step 2

Your pet may sniff out of curiosity. If so, click and reward each time he or she moves toward your hand. Do not reward for licking. Some dogs love to lick, however this command should tell your pet to give a quick nose touch rather than a canine kiss.

Step 3

As your pet catches on, move your hand further away before giving the command. Always keep your hand stationary after issuing a touch command when training. Your dog shouldn't have to chase your hand to touch it. Your pet may become discouraged if you essentially move the goal post each time he or she reaches for it. Eventually you can get your dog to follow your hand movements, but not until he or she fully grasps the meaning of touch.

Caladesi successfully touches owner Allan's hand

Touch Training Tips

If your pet is having trouble understanding, try taking a treat, piece of lunch meat or cheese and smear its scent on your palm. If your dog wasn't interested before, he or she will be now.

Only use the food scent early on if your pet is having difficulties. Some dogs will pick up the basics of touch quickly while others may have a harder time and require a little motivation.

Do not continue to use the food scent after your pet successfully grasps touch. This command is very simple and is best utilized as a way to move your pet in a direction or guide your pet into more complex commands. That means that it is a stepping stone deserving of praise, but not a big step that requires a big reward every time.

Chapter 3
Teaching the Release Command

The release command is another all-purpose trick that can make training sessions much easier. This command simply tells your dog that it's OK to stop what he or she is doing. For example, if you tell your dog to go to his or her kennel and leave the kennel door open, then saying "release" will tell your dog that it is alright to leave the kennel now. This command literally releases your pet from the obligations of your last command.

Step 1

It is difficult to train release without getting your pet to perform another command first. This will be used frequently with stay, kennel, lay and bow so try teaching one of those commands prior to release. Prepare by getting your dog into one of the previously mentioned positions. Simpler commands like sit or stay work best.

Step 2

When you are ready for your dog to break his or her current position, give an enthusiastic "release." Your dog may not understand and will likely only look at you the first few times. To explain the meaning of release to your pet, try encouraging playtime with a toy or playful gestures.

Step 3

Click and praise when your dog successfully releases. Practice this and make sure you apply it to all future training sessions. Your dog should not break a stationary command until you say release.

Mixed breed Dragon responds to the release command by exiting his kennel

Release Training Tips

Avoid overexciting your dog when convincing him or her to play early in release training.

Always be consistent and use release each time you want your dog to stop the current command, even if you are not working through a training session.

Apply the release command all the time, even if your pet has not officially learned it yet. This can help condition him or her to the command.

Chapter 4
Teaching the Sit Command

Sit is usually one of the first commands a new dog owner teaches a puppy. It's very basic, and can help canines learn good manners. The sit command allows you to get your dog into a calm, relaxed position that permits him or her to focus on you. It can also give your pet something else to do instead of jumping up on you, furniture or guests.

Step 1

Get your dog into a standing position. Some dogs will try to sit or lay down. Do not reward this behavior unless you have specifically given the command for it. If your dog continues to sit, simply reposition by taking a step or two backwards so he or she is standing again.

Mixed breed Tiberius prepares for sit

Step 2

Give the sit command. If your dog does it naturally, then click and reward. If not, then show your pet how to do it by raising your hand over his or her head. Perform the gesture slowly so he or she can easily follow the motion. Line your movement up with your pet's current position, as though you are petting your dog over the head and down the middle of the back without actually touching. You should be well over your dog's head so no contact is being made at this point. This is likely to get your dog's attention because it is a new motion that you probably haven't done before.

Tiberius begins to lower his hindquarters in response to the sit command

Step 3

Dogs usually sit down naturally when they look up. As your dog watches your hand his or her rear end will likely hit the ground. As soon as this happens, click and praise. Timing is extremely important to let your pet know that the right action has been taken.

Tiberius sits successfully

Sit Training Tips

If your dog lowers his or her rear but doesn't manage to sit all the way down, click and praise anyway. Time it so that the click occurs as your pet's hindquarters are moving towards the ground.

Scent bait is not recommended for this trick like it was for the touch command. If your pet thinks you have a treat, he or she may stand up or turn around rather than sit to simply watch your hand. This is especially important if your pet responds strongly to food rewards.

As a last resort, try applying light pressure to your dog's hindquarters with your free hand as you attempt to teach the sit command. Many dogs will not require this extra step, but those that are having difficulties may catch on quicker with a little more guidance.

Chapter 5
Teaching the Lay Command

The lay command should come after sit. Sit will give you a way to get your pet in a position that lets him or her shift easily into a laying position. Remember to click and reward as soon as your pet is lying down and not a second later.

Step 1

Get your dog into the sit position. If he or she tries to move, simply reapply the sit command and make eye contact.

Thibor in the sit position

Step 2

Point your finger at the ground near your pet's front paws. He or she will most likely bend down to see what you are pointing at. If your pet moves towards the ground, click and reward.

Step 3

Gradually move your hand along the ground, away from your pet in a smooth, slow motion. Your pet will need to lower his or her front half to follow the gesture.

Thibor lowers his front half in response to the lay command

Step 4

Remember to click and reward each time your pet moves towards the ground until he or she is in the proper lay position. Practice by taking a step or two back, calling your pet to you and repeating the process.

Step 5

Remove the sit command from the equation as your pet learns lay. The goal is to get your pet to execute the action with a single command. Once he or she gets it, simply point at the ground and say lay.

Thibor relaxes in the lay position

Lay Training Tips

Once your pet gets the lay command, try to make him or her hold it for longer periods. This will teach your pet that he or she is to remain lying down until you say otherwise.

Food scent should only be used as a last resort when training this command. Your pet may learn that lay means "chase the yummy hand" which could make it difficult to convince your pet to lie in one place, even after you have walked away.

As with most commands, position yourself in front of your pet. Do not move around while teaching the command. Doing so may distract your dog and cause him or her to stand or try to follow you. Save this type of distraction for later when your pet knows the command well.

Chapter 6
Teaching the Paw Command

Paw is not as practical as many of the other commands covered in this guide, but it is a fun and simple trick to teach your pet. There are a number of variations on the command word that you can consider using, such as "shake", "give me five" or "give paw."

Step 1

Have your dog prepare by sitting. It is often easier to work on this command after your pet has fully grasped sit. Slowly pick up your pet's paw, only a few inches off the ground, and hold it in your hand gently as you say the command. Repeat a few times, saying the command clearly.

Step 2

Put your pet's paw down and hold your hand out, giving the command again. Keep your hand close to your pet's paw. If your pet doesn't seem to understand right away, try a light tap on the top of his or her paw. As soon as you tap, immediately put your hand back into the paw-receiving position.

Owner Allan reaches out while giving Caladesi the paw command

Step 3

Repeat this process, giving a click and reward each time your dog lifts his or her paw. Once your pet has successfully completed the paw command a few times, try lifting your receiving hand higher so your pet has to lift his or her paw higher. Make sure the receiving hand stays at a level that is comfortable for your dog based on his or her size. The dog should be able to easily give you a paw without jumping up.

Caladesi raises her leg in response to the paw command

Paw Training Tips

If your pet becomes confused as you lift your hand further away, simply hold your receiving hand closer and gradually work towards moving it away again.

Once your pet responds to paw, practice the command with an open hand as well as a closed one. Randomly enclose your pet's paw with your hand and give a shake. Other times, keep your finger's spread, more like a high five. This will familiarize your pet with the different ways some people may handle his or her paw.

Practice holding your dog's paw for varying lengths of time. Quickly drop it sometimes while holding on for several seconds other times. This will teach your pet to remain in the position until the paw is let go.

Chapter 7
Teaching the Bow Command

The bow command is a fun addition to your dog's trick list. The bow position is very similar to the dog's natural play position, with the front half lowered and head near the floor while the dog's rear is raised. The difference is that the bow can be done on command and allows you to get your dog to hold this position for a longer period of time. It can make for some adorable photo opportunities!

Step 1

Your pet must be in a standing position to begin the bow. Some dogs will try to sit or lay instead. That is normal. When this happens, simply get your dog standing again and start over. Taking a few steps away and calling your dog to you is usually sufficient to get him or her to stand up again.

Nathan waits in a standing position

Step 2

Working closely with your dog, glide your hand along the ground in front of his or her paws just like you did when training the lay command. This time, also apply gentle pressure between his or her shoulder blades with the fingers on your other hand. Give the bow command while doing this.

Nathan lowers his front half in response to the bow command

Step 3

Do not push down too hard, but apply enough pressure that your dog can feel it. Each time your dog lowers his or her front half, click and praise. Repeat this process until your dog's elbows touch the ground.

Step 4

Practice the bow until your dog can do it without any pressure applied to his or her back. Also work on getting your dog to hold the position for longer periods. This command isn't like the stay command, which you might use to get your pet to remain in one spot for many minutes. However your dog should become accustomed to staying in the bow position until you say otherwise.

Nathan completes a graceful bow

Bow Training Tips

If your dog needs a little incentive, try applying food scent to your hand as you slide it along the ground. This should be done sparingly, but it may get your dog to follow more quickly. Food scent generally works in this instance because your second hand guides your dog's front half downwards, discouraging him or her from trying to walk away.

Practice holding the bow while doing different things. Walk a circle close to your dog and try moving away or making some kind of noise. The better your dog gets at bowing the more distractions you can apply.

Once your pet responds well to the bow command, try getting other people to tell your dog to bow. This is a good practice with every command, but it is especially helpful with this one since the bow tends to be an appealing trick for visitors to see in action.

Chapter 8
Teaching the Kennel Command

The "kennel" command is a practical communication tool that can make life easier for you and your pet. This command tells your dog that it is time to go in the kennel or wherever their confined space is. Kennel allows the owner to quickly and effortlessly get their pet where they need them to be before leaving home, going to bed or starting an activity that requires the family pet to be kept safely out of the way.

Step 1

Bring your dog to his or her kennel. It is often best to start out where you would normally put the kennel on a regular basis. After that, you can practice with other kennels or in other areas. As seen in the photo below, Dragon understands the kennel command even though his kennel is not where it usually is.

Make sure the kennel door is open. Don't start too far away from the kennel. A few steps are sufficient for the first training sessions.

Dragon waits for the kennel command

Step 2

Give the kennel command (or whatever variation you plan to use, some owners prefer "bed") and point to the kennel. Some dogs will go in right away, sometimes out of curiosity or because they already recognize the kennel as their space. Each time the dog moves in the right direction, give a click and reward. If the dog moves away from the kennel, simply get him or her back into position and repeat.

Dragon responds to the kennel command

Step 3

Work towards getting your pet to go in from further away. Avoid using bait, such as a toy or treat, to convince your pet to go in. This will send the wrong message to the dog. A successfully executed kennel command will include the dog going into the kennel with only your spoken word as the incentive.

Dragon looks out from inside his open kennel

Kennel Training Tips

Don't close the kennel door each time your dog goes inside. Leave it open so your pet learns that kennel means to stay in confinement regardless of physical barriers. When you do close the door, do so calmly and quietly.

Randomly kennel your dog for varying periods of time throughout the day. If you only use the command before work, your pet will only learn this habit and not the command. He or she may become reluctant to go in the kennel knowing that it means you are leaving for hours at a time.

Do different things while your pet is in the kennel. If you only kennel your dog while vacuuming, he or she will associate the vacuum with the kennel. Change things up by watching TV, cleaning, or simply leaving the room for a while.

Chapter 9
Teaching the Stay Command

Stay can be a tricky but necessary command. This command will tell your dog that he or she needs to remain in place until you give another command. The stay command is a necessity when taking your pet out into the world or when working towards good off leash behavior.

Mixed breed Faethor waits for his next command

Step 1

Get your pet in a sitting position. Point at him or her and give the "stay" command. If your pet remains still for several seconds, give a click and praise. Keep in mind the time frame for stay will be much shorter at this stage. You can work on a longer stay later so don't expect too much at this point.

Faethor stays in a sitting position

Step 2

Repeat step one until your dog seems comfortable with remaining stationary when the command is given. At this point you can begin to widen the gap between you and your dog. Give the command and take a step or two away. If your dog stays then give another click and reward. If not, put him or her back in the original location and repeat.

Step 3

Continue to widen the distance between you and your pet. Don't rush this phase. Your dog can grasp the stay command in a day, but more time and training will be needed before he or she is comfortable with staying for longer periods or when the distance between you increases.

Stay Training Tips

Never work on the stay command outdoors without a leash unless you have a confined yard with no safety or escape concerns.

Always put your dog back where you originally placed him or her if the stay command is not followed. Do not allow your dog to inch closer to you by disobeying the command.

As your dog gets good at stay, begin adding distractions. Practice by walking in different directions around your dog. Perform various activities like throwing an enticing ball or sitting on the ground. This gets your pet used to staying in position no matter what you are doing or where you go.

Even if your dog becomes a stay pro, it is not recommended that pet owners allow their canines to run off leash in a public setting. There are many risks and uncontrollable variables that can be a danger, even to the most obedient dog.

Chapter 10
Teaching the Heel Command

The heel command is an excellent tool when taking your dog out into the world. Heel helps you communicate with your pet and makes him or her much more pleasant to walk.

Step 1

Put your dog on leash and bring him or her to your left side. Begin in a sitting position, so your left leg and your dog's front right leg are parallel.

Nathan waits for the heel command

Step 2

Get your hands into position. This involves holding the end of the leash in your right hand. If the leash has a loop like most do, then loop it around your right wrist. Grasp near the middle of the leash with your left hand so some of the slack is dangling in front of you. Make sure your pet has a little slack as well so he or she doesn't feel constant tension or pulling. There shouldn't be so much slack that your dog can get far away from or possibly trip you.

Step 3

Give the heel command and slowly step forward with your left foot. Never pull on the leash and keep your gait and posture as it normally would be when walking without your dog. Do not bend down or pull your dog along. Focus on walking naturally with your pet.

Nathan heels while on an outdoor walk

Step 4

If your pet stays by your left side, click and reward. Continue walking for as long as your pet will obey. If your pet breaks the heel position, start over with him or her sitting at your left side again and repeat the process.

Step 5

Practice heeling with your pet on the same side. Be sure to take random turns and change your pace occasionally as your dog gets comfortable. This teaches your pet to pay attention to what you are doing at all times while on the leash. As your pet improves, you can increase the heel duration and begin to introduce distractions.

Nathan smiles while he heels

Heel Training Tips

Consider training your dog to sit each time you stop moving when performing heel. This puts your pet in a comfortable position where he or she is less inclined to try and roam around while you stop to chat or do something stationary on a walk. Give the sit command each time you pause, but eventually eliminate the spoken sit command so your dog simply does it each time your feet stop moving.

If your pet doesn't seem to be paying attention to you when training heel, try a few sharp turns. Never drag or jerk your dog, but make an abrupt left or right turn that forces your dog to regroup and follow your lead. This reminds your pet to pay attention to you and move as a single unit.

Nathan displays what not to do by stopping to smelling a pretty distraction

If you are training an older or larger dog that pulls, consider using a choke chain for this command. The dog will be less likely to pull if the choke chain is used properly.

Get your dog in the habit of only walking with you when heeling. That means your dog should not be sniffing around exploring or using the potty when heeling. Give your pet an opportunity to use their potty area prior to practicing heel or going on walks. If your pet tries to sniff or do something other than walk with you, simply keep moving.

Chapter 11
Troubleshooting

Your dog may get some commands quickly while others may require many repetitions. The instructions in this guide can teach your dog the basics of the command, but it is up to you to practice each day so your pet gets good at it. If you are having trouble training, consider the following:

If your dog seems too anxious or excited to pay attention, make sure you work in separate play time and exercise sessions. Let your dog burn off excess energy then ask him or her to pay attention.

Just like humans, dogs learn at different speeds. If your dog seems confused by a command, simply go back and perform the last steps he or she already knows before trying to progress again.

Frustration can cause a dog to lose interest in training sessions. If you sense frustration, practice a few of the commands your pet knows well. Alternate between these and more difficult commands to keep your pet motivated.

Left: Nathan is distracted by pedestrians while walking

Is your dog paying more attention to the things around him or her than to you during training? This could be an indication that your chosen training area is not ideal. Cut down on distractions – that should include the things your pet can hear, see, touch and smell.

Does your pet act eager at first but becomes less interested as the training session progresses? Reduce the length of each session so your dog is comfortable with the duration. Gradually increase the duration if you want to, however keep in mind that shorter sessions often work better overall.

Training Everyday

Training shouldn't end once your dog understands the commands you want him or her to know. Without practice, your dog can begin to forget or become less responsive. Go through your dog's command list each day. This doesn't have to be a formal process. Simply give a command whenever you want as practice. Your pet will love having something to engage his or her mind and you can strengthen the bond you share as canine and human pack leader.

If you want your dog to become a well behaved obedience pro, make a point to practice each command in a different setting with unique distractions. A relaxed social gathering is a great opportunity to show off your pet's skills while improving his or her responsiveness.

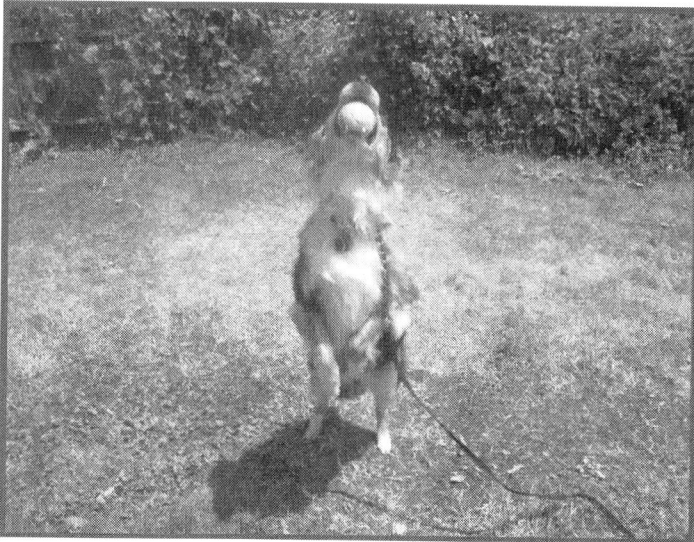

Caladesi catches her favorite toy

Your dog is an individual, so tailor your training approach to his or her needs and abilities. You may not realize this but your dog really wants to work with you and be a part of your life. Training is another way to rediscover your unique bond and spend time together. Give your pet a little time each day and he or she will show you what amazing things a trained dog can do!

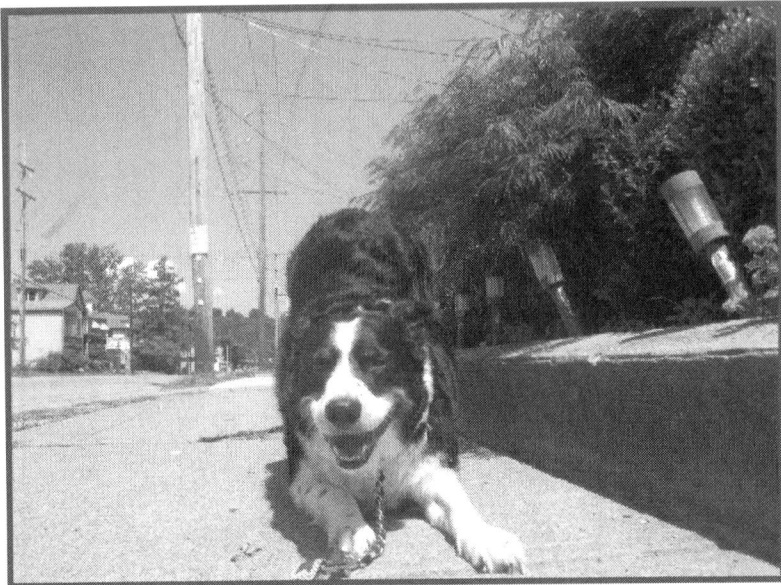

Nathan wishes you and your dog obedience training success!